I0429621

Pioneer

Free Will Baptists

Ministers

Burial Locations

In

Virginia

This book was printed in the United States of America.

To order additional copies of this book, contact:
FWB Publications
Enchanting Acres
1006 Rayme Drive
Columbus, Ohio 43207
Alton.loveless@prodigy.net
Or
www.amazon.com

FWB
FWB Publications

Introduction
Virginia

This book represents all that were part of the Free Will Baptist movement, consisting of the Palmer (south), Randall (north) and others such as the Stone, John-Thomas, John Wheeler Assns., NC OFWB and more.

Many of the photos are poor quality, but it was all I could find. Likewise, I do not have photos or tombstones for many of them. The information about these ministers were all that was available to me or found in archives. I made every effort to include those for which they would be remembered. Some I had no information, but research had shown they were of our denomination.

This Section is taken for a two Volume set done by this author.

Virginia

Hobert Monroe Addington
Birth:
Apr. 11, 1919
Wise,
Wise County, Virginia
Death:
Oct. 6, 2008
Wise,
Wise County, Virginia
Burial:
Wise Cemetery, Wise,
Wise County, Virginia

Rev. Hobert Monroe Addington lived to the age of 89. He was a member of the Esserville Freewill Baptist Church, a pastor for several Freewill Baptist churches in the area, a member of the UMWA and was an employee of Old Ben Coal Co. for over 33 years.

Howard T Bostic
Birth:
May 31, 1905
Swords Creek,
Russell County, Virginia
Death:
Jul. 4, 1987
Swords Creek,
Russell County, Virginia
Burial:
Bostic Call Cemetery,
Swords Creek
,Russell County, Virginia

Rev James A. Boatright
Birth:
Mar. 30, 1891
Scott County
Virginia
Death:
Dec. 31, 1982
Burial:
Carter Cemetery
Scott County
Virginia

WW I Veteran, and a minister in the Free Will Baptist church.

Robert Franklin Breeden
Birth:
April 8, 1927
Buena Vista Rockbridge County
Virginia
Death:
January 13, 2016
Buena Vista Rockbridge County
Virginia
Burial:
Green Hill Cemetery
Buena Vista City
Virginia

Rev. Robert F. Breeden, 88, passed at home on Wednesday, in the town of his birth, Buena Vista, Virginia. Known to many as "Bob" and "Pastor Breeden", he was a retired ordained minister. He was a veteran of World War II and the Korean Conflict and served his country in the Navy, Marine Corps, and Army. He retired from the US Army in 1968 at the rank of Major. He pastored Free Will Baptist churches in North Carolina, New Hampshire, Maine, Tennessee, Wisconsin, Maryland and Virginia.

He was married to Zalene Boone Lloyd on November 27, 1954 in her hometown of Durham, North Carolina. She died in December of 2004, a few weeks after celebrating their 50th wedding anniversary. Bob and Zalene adopted four children between 1956 and 1967.

Rev. Breeden is preceded in death by his parents, James Franklin & Carrie White (Sprouse) Breeden; seven brothers and sisters; his wife, Zalene Lloyd; and his son, Kenneth Wayne Breeden. He is survived by younger brother Edward Lyle Breeden; his son Wade Franklin (Terri), a daughter Rebecca (Breeden) Wentworth (Randal), his son Jonathan Russell Breeden; and seven grandchildren, Lance, Shannon, Brent, Dane, Hunter, Randal and Quent; and two great-grandchildren, Jenson and Madalyn.

The funeral was at the Bolling Grose & Lotts Funeral Home located at 2160 East Midland Trail in Buena Vista, Virginia at 11:00 am. The Rev. Stanley Waddell, pastor of Woodland Heights FWB Church of Martinsville officiating.

Missionary Zalene Lloyd Breeden
Birth:
Jun. 22, 1916 Durham, Durham
County,
North Carolina
Death:
Dec. 14, 2004
Buena Vista, Rockbridge County,
Virginia
Burial: Green Hill Cemetery, Buena
Vista,
Rockbridge County, Virginia

At the age of 32, and single, she boarded with Dan and Trula Cronk on August 8, 1948 for India assigned by the Free Will Baptists missionary board to work with Laura Belle Barnard who had been in India several years. Midway through her term she resigned as a Free Will Baptist missionary and to work for Dr. Graham's homes in Kalimpong, West Bengal, situated in the Himalayan foothills in Northeast India. On her return back to the United States another classmate Marie Hanna and her husband were beginning their service in India.

On November 27, 1954, she married Robert F. Breeden, to whom she would become a devoted wife, mother, homemaker and pastor's wife. Afterwards, serving as a home missionary and pastor's wife in North Carolina, New Jersey, Alaska, New Hampshire, Maine, Wisconsin, Tennessee and Virginia. They celebrated their 50th wedding anniversary on November 27, 2004.

She was a graduate of Free Will Baptist Bible college in Nashville, Tennessee and Nyack college, Nyack, New York.

Gird Ashby Cave
Birth:
Mar. 16, 1884
Madison County
Virginia
Death:
Jul. 10, 1972
Burial:
Victory Baptist Church Cemetery
Comertown

Page County, Virginia

Rev. Gird Ashby Cave, 88, of Comertown died at home after a lingering illness. He had been a frequent patient in Harrisonburg and Luray hospitals. Mr. Cave was a preacher at Comertown's Independent Church and a country store merchant 35 years in Comertown. He was well-known throughout the county as a preacher, frequently heard on local radio stations and conducting street corner services in Luray. He was a son of the late John Isaac and Mary Katherine Offenbacker Cave. His wife the former Dorothy Ann Thomas. The couple celebrated their 67th wedding 10isconsin10y Dec 26.

John A Cave
Birth:
1812
Death:
Nov., 1899
Burial:
Calvin H Cave Cemetery
Mauck
Page County, Virginia

He was an early minister in Virginia. is Wife was Mary Ann Phillips Cave who he married on August 31, 1835 in Virginia.

Waymond Larson Cave, Sr
Birth:
Aug. 4, 1933
Death:
Jan. 24, 1994
Burial:
Victory Baptist Church Cemetery
Comertown
Page County, Virginia

Rev. Cave died at age 60. He was pastor of the Comertown FWB Church in Shenandoah. He was ordained in Nov. 1, 1969. He was the co-founder of the Comertown church where he pastored for 25 years until his health failed. He played the guitar and sang gospel songs with his father and much of his encouragement came from his grandfather, Rev. G.A. Cave who gave the property for the church and who preached for 67 years before his death. His parents were Ralph William Cave and Elsie Lillian Breeden Cave.

John Colby
Birth:

Dec. 10, 1787
Death:
Nov. 30, 1817
Burial:
Saint Paul's Episcopal Churchyard,
Norfolk,
Norfolk City, Virginia

At age 30 Years he died while on a long preaching trip to Ohio and was on his way back home to Vermont. He died in Norfork, Va. Is in buried in a quaint gravesite near the Episcopal Church. His ministry, while short, touched many lives and many came to Christ a list of ministers accepted the call to preach became of him. A memorial to him is in the Sutton Village cemetery at Sutton, Vermont. He was a very talented rising star and mourned by his denomination when he died. A autobiography of his life was written and published by Free Will Baptists.

Samuel Brack Combs
BIRTH
12 Aug 1906
DEATH
7 Sep 1948 (aged 42)
BURIAL
Comers Creek Baptist Church
Cemetery
Troutdale, Grayson County,
Virginia

Samuel Brack Combs was a fast, hard Pentecostal style preacher. He was crushed in the coal mines.

Albert Dingus

Birth:
Mar. 3, 1945
Death:
Feb. 25, 2008
Burial:
Laurel Grove Cemetery,
Norton,Wise County, Virginia

He bgan preaching in October 1927 with Ben and Wade Powers at the FWB church on Mudtown Hill in Jenkins, Kentucky. He was ordained on April 21, 1928. He and 8 other believers organized the Burdine Free Will Baptist Church in Jenkins. For over 56 years he was the faithful and loving pastor of that church. His ledger contained more than a 1000 names of those he baptized, married and held funeral. In 1936 he was instrumental in organizing the Letcher County Conference of FWB which united with the John Thomas Association. More that 50 men surrendered to preach under his ministry. At a Bible Conference held at FWBBC in Nashville, Tenn. In 1982, he was asked to stand and was acknowledged as one of the outstanding pastors among Free Will Baptists.

Robert Aston Dingus
Birth:
Jul. 13, 1883

Virginia
Death:
Feb. 21, 1951
Virginia
Burial:
Sabras Chapel Cemetery,
Dungannon,
Scott County, Virginia
World War I Draft

Harley Graham Dye, Sr

Birth:
Sep. 30, 1903
Swords Creek
Russell County, Virginia
Death:
Oct. 25, 1993
Oak Ridge
Anderson County, Tennessee
Burial:
Greenhills Memory Gardens
Claypool Hill
Tazewell County, Virginia

He was a FWB preacher for 45 years conducting revivals and pastor numerous churches in the John-Thomas Association. He served on the New Durm Ordaining Council was a member and Honorary Pastor of the East Lebanon FWB church.

James Edward Dye

Birth:
Jun. 16, 1921
Drill
Russell County, Virginia
Death:
Nov. 5, 2011

Oakwood
Buchanan County, Virginia

Burial:
Haywood Wilson Cemetery
Swords Creek
Russell County, Virginia

Rev. James Edward Dye, age , 90, spent his early life in Drill, moving to Buchanan County in 1940. A United States Army veteran, serving serving in Europe during World War II. A retired coal miner, And a member of UMWA Local 2372 in Jewell Valley. He was a member of Guiding Light Free Will Baptist Church and had been a minister for over 60 years In the John-Thomas Association. Military honors were conducted by VFW Post 9864 of Lebanon, Virginia.

Finas "Bud" Arlin Hill

Birth:
Nov. 22, 1936
Death:
Aug. 10, 2002
Burial:
Hill Family Cemetery
Haysi
Dickenson County, Virginia

He was a minister in the Dickenson County Conference Of the John-Thomas Association, for 22 years. He was a member of Splashdam Freewill Baptist Church in Haysi and Pastor of Phillips Chapel freewill Baptist Church in West Dante.He worked for Chevrolet's Warren, Mich., plant for 14 years, a member of UAW Local No. 909. He worked for Island Creek Coal Comoany's No. 1 mine for 19 years and was a member of UMWA Local No. 1509.

Joseph Edgar Holden
Birth:
Jan. 1, 1869
Death:
Oct. 26, 1927
Burial:
Mayo Baptist Church Cemetery
Spencer
Henry County, Virginia
He was a member of the John Wheeler Association which helped its seventh anniversary on September 1, 1887 this Association had churches or were located in the extreme northwest part of North Carolina and the northeast part of Tennessee, with his territory extending northward even into Virginia. Rev. Holden was a member of this large body of Free Will Baptists.

Rev Lester D Horton
BIRTH
10 Mar 1930
Tennessee, USA

DEATH
24 Jun 2019 (aged 89)
Front Royal, Warren County, Virginia, USA

BURIAL
Stonewall Memory Gardens
Manassas, Manassas City, Virginia,

Well known pastor in Fairfax, Virginia who was active in denominational affairs.

Monroe Hubbard
Birth:
Dec. 4, 1883
Death:
Apr. 10, 1977
Burial:
Dewey Memorial Cemetery,
Wise County, Virginia

Kyle Wilson Hubbard
Birth:
1902
Death:
March 4, 1990
Bristol, Virginia
Burial:
Russell Memorial Cemetery
Lebanon
Russell County, Virginia

He was a faithful member of the
Tunnel HIll Free Will Baptist Church
where he was ordained into the
ministry in The John-Thomas
Association, November, 1940 at
this church and at the time of his
death was the pastor emeritus.

Rev James Wesley Hunnicutt
Birth
16 Oct 1814
South Carolina
Death
8 Oct 1880
Stafford County, Virginia
Burial
Fredericksburg emetery
Fredericksburg,
Fredericksburg City, Virginia
Plot
Section 6, Lot 62,
Stone 17

An ardent Unionist, Hunnicutt was editor of the Christian Banner newspaper in Fredericksburg at the outbreak of the war. He was forced to suspend publication during the first year of the war, then resumed publication for several months in 1862, but fled Fredericksburg under threat of death before the Confederate occupation in late 1862, spending the reminder of the war in Philadelphia.

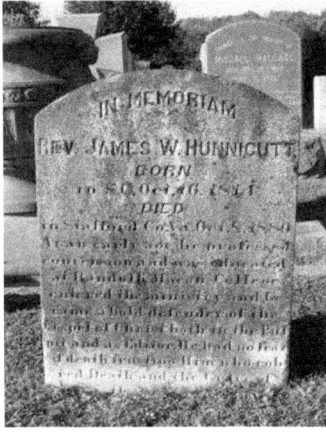

Ezra Johnson
Birth:
Feb. 19, 1916
Dickenson County, Virginia
Death:
Dec. 19, 1986
Burial:
Dewey Memorial Cemetery

Wise County, Virginia

He was a Free Will Baptist Preacher For Almost 50 Years And He Loved To sing and taught sing and to anyone who wanted to learn. He taught all of his children to sing and he baptized and married six of them.

Emmett J Kilgore, Jr
Birth:
Aug. 8, 1914
Death:
Nov. 12, 2001
Burial:
Greenwood Memorial Gardens,
Coeburn,
Wise County,
Virginia

Harold Kilgore
Birth:
Feb. 13, 1931
Death:
Dec. 4, 1999
Wise,
Wise County, Virginia
Burial:
Wise Cemetery,
Wise
Wise County,

Virginia

He was a bi-vocational Free Will Baptist minister and was a book keeper for a large mining concern. His two sons also became FWB ministers as well.

James Patton Lambert
Birth:
Oct. 25, 1904
Death:
Mar. 11, 1983
Abingdon
Washington County, Virginia
Burial:
Sullivan Cemetery
Bee, Dickenson County, Virginia

He was a FWB and a member of the John-Thomas Association

William Henry Large
Birth:
Dec. 30, 1861
Hawkins County, Tennessee
Death:
Sep. 10, 1951
Blountville,
Sullivan County, Tennessee
Burial:
Johnson Cemetery,
Washington County, Virginia

Rev. Vergel Maness
Birth:
Jan. 30, 1887
Death:
February 8, 2018
Burial:
Westhampton Memorial Park.
Virginia

Vergel Amos Maness, 80, was the son of the late Loice and Martha Maness and was preceded in death by his daughter, Katherine Maness; and his brother, Jonney Maness. He is survived by his loving wife, Alyne Maness; sons, Jonathen and Vergel; grandchildren, Vergel Allen Maness, Joshua Pritt, Benjamin Pritt, Christopher Pritt, Kayla Maness, Ryan Maness and Emily Maness;

Before full retirement, Brother Vergel most recently served as an associate at First Free Will Baptist Church, Richmond. He has been a pastor as well as a church planter through the Free Will Baptist National Home Missions Department.

S. M. McFall, Sr
Birth:
Jan. 30, 1887
Death:
Jan. 8, 1977
Burial:
Kilgore Cemetery,
Banner, Wise County, Virginia

Ordained a Freewill Baptist Minister, in Nov 1910 by Elders W. R. Stallard, Cain Counts, and John Pennel.

Vester McKinney
Birth:
Nov. 15, 1901
Death:
Mar. 21, 1989
Tazewell County, Virginia
Burial:
Ramsey Cemetery
Clinchco
Dickenson County,
Virginia

He was a former employee of the WM Ritter lumber company, a retired coal miner, a minister of the Free Will Baptist denomination for 45 years In the John-Thomas Association, and a United States Army veteran.

Ersel McPeek
Birth:
Oct. 17, 1908
Death:
Sep. 18, 1994
Burial:
Dewey Memorial Cemetery
Wise County, Virginia

He was a member of the John-Thomas Assn. and a FWB preacher.

STORE UP YOUR TREASURES IN HEAVEN

Daniel James Merkh, Sr
Birth:
1928

Death:
Apr. 12, 2002
Burial:
Holly Lawn Cemetery,
Suffolk,
Suffolk City,
Virginia

He was a student at the Free Will Baptist Bible college in Nashville, Tennessee and after his graduation he and his wife, Margaret, were commissioned in 1957 as missionaries. Rev. Merkh and family spent one year in Lausanne, Switzerland to learn the French language, four years in the Ivory Coast of West Africa and nine and a half years in France as missionaries.

After these times of service, they retired from foreign mission service in 1975. He was both a teacher and church planter on the mission field Rev. Merkh, a native of Camden, N.J., also served as a pastor in Tennessee, South Carolina and Virginia for 20 years and lastly serving the First Free Will Baptist Church in, Richmond, Virginia where he retired. He was a member of Ryanwood Free Will Baptist Church, Vero Beach, Florida. and a veteran of the U.S. Marines during World War II.

Missionary Margaret Lucille *Johnson* Merkh
Birth:
Jan. 29, 1930
Death:
Feb. 21, 2012
Burial:
Holly Lawn Cemetery
Suffolk Suffolk City, Virginia,

She was predeceased by her husband of 54 years, Rev. Daniel James Merkh, Sr. Rev. Merkh, Margaret, and family spent one year in Lausanne, Switzerland to learn the French language, four years in the Ivory Coast of West Africa, and nine and half years in France as missionaries. After returning to the United States, Margaret later went on to work and retired as an executive secretary for Dominion Power. She was a member of the Free Will Baptist Church in Carrollton, Virginia.

Ben Powers

Birth:
Unknown
Death:
1983
Virginia
Burial:
Temple Hill Memorial Park
Castlewood
Russell County, Virginia

His lineage was from a circuit riding Methodist preacher background. He helped organize 23 Free Will Baptist Churches in the 1940's in Wise County, Va. And portions of Kentucky. He and his brother Wade Powers were used in numerous revivals in surrounding counties. They would stay with people in the community for two to three weeks at a time, from house to house, and then preach revivals during the evening hours. They would receive poundings of food items as honorariums.

David D. Powers, Sr
Birth:
Jul. 17, 1920

Death:
Sep. 3, 1993
Burial:
Laurel Grove Cemetery,
Norton,
Wise County,
Virginia

Inscription: PFC US Army World War II

Harlis H Powers
BIRTH
12 Mar 1927
DEATH
5 Dec 2006 (aged 79)
BURIAL
Round Top Cemetery
Wise, Wise County, Virginia, USA

Free Will Baptist preacher and US Army WW II

He and his brother Ben Powers were used in numerous revivals in surrounding counties. He preached as far as Louisa, Kentucky. They would stay with people in the community for two to three weeks at a time, from house to house and then preach revivals during the evening hours.

Rev Rueben H Powers
Birth:
Jun. 26, 1855
Scott County
Virginia
Death:
Jan. 14, 1922
Wise County
Virginia
Burial:
Round Top Cemetery
Wise
Wise County,Virginia
A Free Will Baptist minister in Wise Co. Virginia. Son of George and Katherine Kennedy Powers

Wade H Powers, Sr
Birth:
1894
Death:
1970
Burial:
Perry Cemetery,
Wise,
Wise County,
Virginia

Eli E. Reedy
Birth:
1879
Death:
1950
Burial:
Clinch Valley Memorial Cemetery
Richlands,
Tazewell County, Virginia

Howard Reynolds
Birth:
Mar. 29, 1925
Russell County, Virginia
Death:
Dec. 19, 2007
Lebanon
Russell County, Virginia
Burial:
Reynolds Family Cemetery
Honaker
Russell County, Virginia

Reynolds, 82,of Honaker, was a lifelong resident of Russell County, and a member and pastor of Tunnell Hill Freewill Baptist Church for 14 years in the John-Thomas Association.

George Wythe Salyers
Birth:
Aug. 1, 1918
Death:
Jan. 4, 1986
Burial:
Rugsby Church Cemetery
Dickenson County,
Virginia

He was a member of the Rachel Chapel Free Will Baptist Church and a minister for 25 years. He served on the ordaining Council for 15 years and served as pastor of the Yates Chapel church for 24 years. He was a veteran of World War II having served in the United States Army.

Glen W Stevens
Birth:
May 7, 1917
Virginia
Death:
May 21, 1988
Virginia
Burial:
Bowen Cemetery
Russell County, Virginia

He was a retired coal miner and a member of the Mt. View Freewill Baptist church on Combs Ridge. He was a Free Will Baptist minister With the John-Thomas Association.

mines for 39 years and was a member of the UWMA union. He retired from Bethlehem Steel at the age of 55.

Roy C. Vanover
Birth:
Dec. 5, 1918
Death:
Mar. 25, 2003
Burial:
Powell Valley Memorial Gardens
Big Stone Gap
Wise County,
Virginia

He was called to preach in September 24, 1968 and was ordained on October 25, 1969. He served as pastor of the Pyles Memorial, Ferbie Chapel, and Lone Pine Chapel Of the John-Thomas Association. He was very active in many of the churches throughout the area in his preaching, singing and praying. He was a member of the Lone Pine Chapel. In his early years he sang with the Friendly Four Quartet. He was a member of that Dickenson County conference and was a member of this ordaining Council. He served on the Board of Directors also for Camp Jacob. He worked in the coal

Ralph Edward Vicars
Birth:
Unknown
Death:
Mar. 29, 2009
Norton, Wise County, Virginia
Burial:
Wise Cemetery
Wise,
Wise County, Virginia

He was the pastor of the Burdine Free Will Baptist church

Ralph Lee Weaver
Birth:

Nov. 10, 1915
Kannapolis
Cabarrus County, North Carolina
Death:
Oct. 21, 1992
Durham
Durham County, North Carolina
Burial:
Roselawn Burial Park
Martinsville
Martinsville, Virginia
Plot: 16-245

Rev. Ralph Lee Weaver, 76-year-old pastor of Woodland Heights Free Will Baptist Church, Martinsville, VA, since 1948, died from complications of bypass heart surgery in Duke University Hospital, Durham, NC. He preached his last sermon Sunday morning, Sept. 27th, after suffering chest pains all night. Weaver was the son of Ira Samuel and Margaret Ada (Bullard) Weaver, one of several children. Rev. Weaver served as moderator of the Maryland Association, and was a life member o f the Martinsville/Henry Co. Rescue Squad where he served as as chaplain. His long ministry at Woodland Heights began in 1948, with 12 members where he built the membership until the congregation outgrew their facility and purchased land in 1956 and began a building program in 1959, on the present location.Rev. Weaver was graduated from Martinsville Bible College and attended Patrick Henry Community College.

Harry Paul Whitaker
Birth:
Jul. 27, 1922
Bostic
Rutherford County, North Carolina
Death:
Mar. 29, 1994
Russell County, Virginia
Burial:
Temple Hill Memorial Park
Castlewood
Russell County,
Virginia

He entered the ministry in 1955 and was ordained as a Free Will Baptist minister In the John Thomas Association on November 30, 1957. He dedicated 40 years serving the Straight Hollow Free Will Baptist where he pastored for 22 years.

www.ingramcontent.com/pod-product-compliance
Lightning Source LLC
Chambersburg PA
CBHW072016280526
45788CB00005B/2070